KARATE

Clive Gifford

SEA-TO-SEA
Mankato Collingwood London

This edition first published in 2011 by
Sea-to-Sea Publications
Distributed by Black Rabbit Books
P.O. Box 3263, Mankato, Minnesota 56002

Printed in China, Dongguan

Library of Congress Cataloging-in-Publication Data

Gifford, Clive.
  Karate / Clive Gifford.
     p. cm. -- (Combat sports)
  Includes index.
  ISBN 978-1-59771-275-0 (library binding)
  1. Karate--Juvenile literature. I. Title.
  GV1114.3.G55 2011
  796.815'3--dc22

                        2009051537

9 8 7 6 5 4 3 2

Published by arrangement with the Watts Publishing Group Ltd, London.

Series editor: Adrian Cole
Art director: Jonathan Hair
Design: Big Blu
Cover design: Peter Scoulding
Picture research: Luped Picture Research

Acknowledgments:
Bandphoto / uppa.co.uk: 9; Columbia / The Kobal Collection: 4, 10; Jamie Squire / Getty Images: 5; Jed Jacobsohn / Getty
Images: 28; Kevin Winter / Getty Images: 11; Lech Muszyński / PAP / Corbis: 15; Lifestyle Photography: 8, 13, 16, 17, 18,
19, 20, 21, 26, 27, 28, 29; Michael S. Yamashita / Corbis: 12; Nadine Rupp / Bongarts / Getty Images: 14;
Paul Gilham / Getty Images: 24; Reuters / Kim Kyung-Hoon: 22; Reuters / Thaier al-Sudani: 23; Roslan Rahman / AFP /
Getty Images: 1, 25. Every attempt has been made to clear copyright. Should there be any
inadvertent omission please apply to the publisher for rectification.

March 2010
RD/6000006414/002

CONTENTS

WHAT IS KARATE?

What combat sport was originally practiced in secret, and has been surrounded in mystery for centuries? Karate, of course!

Empty Hand

The word "karate" comes from the Japanese words *kara* and *te*, which together mean "empty hand." It is a martial art where people use parts of their body, not weapons, to perform movements for exercise, self-defense, and sport.

Karateka

There are now more than 40 million karateka—people who practice karate—around the world. These range from schoolchildren to superstars, including glamorous actresses, such as Lucy Liu and Jenny McCarthy, and Hollywood big-hitters, such as Chuck Norris and Jackie Chan.

Lucy Liu (far left) stars as Alex Munday in Charlie's Angels, alongside Cameron Diaz and Drew Barrymore.

Respect for all Styles

There are many different styles or schools of karate, including Shotokan and Goju-ryu karate. All teach karateka to respect other styles as well as respecting their teachers and classmates.

A ROYAL SPORT

The Crown Prince of the United Arab Emirates and ruler of Dubai, Sheik Mohammad Bin Rashid Al Maktoum, is a karateka. In 2006, his daughter, Maitha (above, left), became the first Arab woman to win a medal in karate at the Asian Games.

KARATE'S ORIGINS

Unlike many combat sports, karate began in one region: Okinawa and the other Ryukyu islands off the south coast of Japan.

No Weapons

In 1477, King Sho Shin banned his people—the islanders of Okinawa—from carrying weapons. This ban continued after the islands were invaded by the Japanese in 1609.

To defend themselves, the islanders practiced forms of unarmed combat, some of which came from Ancient China. Over centuries of practicing in secret, these developed into what we know as karate.

Gichin Funakoshi (fourth from left) poses with other karate masters in the 1930s.

Shoto's Karate

Gichin Funakoshi (1868–1957) was a schoolteacher and poet who wrote under the name Shoto. He had first learned karate in secret on Okinawa during the ban. In 1902, karate was taught in schools for the first time. Funakoshi taught students and became the founder of the Shotokan school of karate.

Big in Japan

Gichin Funakoshi took karate from Okinawa to mainland Japan in 1916. He displayed his skills in demonstrations and impressed many people, including the man who would later become Emperor Hirohito of Japan. Slowly, karate spread through Japan.

Karate demonstrations, such as this one at Shuri Castle, Okinawa, took place throughout Japan in the early twentieth century.

"The ultimate aim of karate lies not in victory or defeat, but in the perfection of the character of its participants."
– *Gichin Funakoshi.*

KARATE SPREADS AROUND THE WORLD

From Japan, Japanese masters and their students traveled all over the world, taking their skills with them.

Teaching Abroad

Starting in the 1950s onward, Gichin Funakoshi's top students began to move abroad to teach karate in the United States and Europe. Keinosuke "Tiger" Enoeda (1935–2003), for example, went to Liverpool, England, in 1965 and formed the Karate Union of Great Britain. He remained in the United Kingdom for the rest of his life.

American Karate

After World War II (1939–45), U.S. soldiers occupied parts of Japan including Okinawa. There, they learned about karate and took their knowledge home with them. Karate schools began to open in the United States.

Keinosuke Enoeda, a 9th-dan black belt, took Shotokan karate to England.

Karate Elvis

The "King" of rock 'n' roll, Elvis Presley (1935–77), first trained in karate in the U.S. Army in 1959. By 1970, he had risen to an 8th-dan black belt (see page 13)—a very high level of karate.

Elvis Presley also starred in movies where he displayed his karate skills—bringing karate to a wider audience.

SCHOOLS OF KARATE

There are four main schools or styles of karate:

✴ Shotokan—Gichin Funakoshi's school of karate, the most common form of karate today.

✴ Goju-ryu—this school has more emphasis on strength training than Shotokan.

✴ Shito-ryu—founded in 1928 by Kenwa Mabuni (1889–1952), this features short, fast movements.

✴ Wado-ryu—created in the early 1930s, this involves holds and some moves taken from another Japanese martial art, ju-jitsu.

"As a student of the martial arts, Elvis was one of the best. He was physically strong and his technique was excellent."
Kang Rhee, Elvis's karate instructor.

KARATE AT THE MOVIES

With its fast moves, it is no surprise that karate has featured in many movies. These range from explosive Asian martial arts movies to family-friendly movies such as *The Karate Kid* series.

In The Karate Kid, *a young boy learns the ways of karate from an old master named Mr. Miyagi. The movie was a huge hit and inspired thousands of people to join karate schools.*

Hong Kong Action

Many action movies showing karate and other martial arts were produced in Japan, China, and especially Hong Kong, in the 1960s and 1970s. Bruce Lee was the biggest star but others, such as karate champions Sonny Chiba and Jackie Chan, went on to make big-budget, blockbuster movies. Many people in Europe and the United States saw the movies and took up karate as a result.

Students Turned Stars

Former students of karate went on to become major action and martial arts movie stars themselves. These include Chuck Norris and Dolph Lundgren, who won European championships in karate in 1980 and 1981.

Super Sonny Chiba

Sonny Chiba played the karate pioneer Masutatsu Oyama in three movies, *Champion of Death* (1975), *Karate Bearfighter* (1975), and *Karate for Life* (1977).

Sonny Chiba, seen here with Lucy Liu, at the opening of a movie in which he played master swordmaker Hattori Hanzo.

AT THE DOJO

Dojo means a sacred space used for karate or other martial arts. Students entering a *dojo* are expected to behave according to the five *dojo kun,* or "rules." Students also wear a special uniform.

These karate students are practicing in a dojo.

Karate Gi

A *gi* is a karate uniform. The jacket and pants are made of strong, hard-wearing cotton. The sleeves and legs of a *gi* are loose to allow lots of freedom of movement. A *gi* must be respected; it is washed and folded when not in use.

THE FIVE DOJO KUN

✹ Seek perfection of character
✹ Be faithful
✹ Endeavor and persevere
✹ Respect others
✹ Refrain from violent behavior

Belting Up

A karate jacket is tied using a large belt, or *obi*. Different-colored *obi* show the level the student has achieved. The color order varies for different schools of karate, but usually beginners start with a white belt and progress up through the colors, often orange, yellow, green, brown, and finally, black. Black belt karateka can continue to progress. They start at 1st dan. The highest level of all is 10th dan.

TIE N' DYE

Gichin Funakoshi borrowed judo's colored belt system in the 1920s and applied it to karate. At first, the white belt that karateka wore was simply dyed a new color. This is the reason why the color of the belts went from light to dark.

A junior karate student has progressed to the next level and is presented with a new obi.

KARATE TODAY

Karate features three major activities. *Kumite* is sparring technique (see pages 22–23). *Kata* and *kihon* are the other two main activities.

Kata

A *kata* is a pattern of moves performed in a row. It can look like a beautiful but deadly dance. *Kata* feature many of the important kicks, punches, and blocks learned in training, mixed with steps and turns. There are more than 100 different types and styles.

Students perform a kata *featuring a low cross block.*

Kihon

Kihon means basic principles and includes learning the movements and positions required for the main strikes, punches, blocks, and kicks. Learning about stances (*dachi*) is an important part of *kihon*. All moves begin from the correct stance, which provides a solid base for balancing.

TAMASHIWARA

The word *tamashiwara* means strength testing by breaking various objects, from ice to concrete. It is rarely a part of karate instruction but is popular on TV and in demonstrations. In September 2007, Ali Bahçetepe from Turkey broke 317 concrete blocks in one minute.

Only highly experienced karateka should attempt tamashiwara. *It requires great mental and physical strength.*

TOP 10 KARATE MOVES 1 – 3

There are many moves in karate but most start from one of the small number of stances. The three moves shown here can all begin from a front stance known as *zenkutsu dachi*.

1 Mae Geri (Front Kick)

Mae geri, or front kick, is a fast kick that is difficult to defend against. The karateka raises his knee to waist height then snaps his lower leg forward, with the foot pointing forward but the toes pulled back. The striking area is the ball of the foot. The hips are thrust forward to add speed to the kick with the other leg bent to help balance.

2 Oi-Zuki (Lunge Punch)

Oi-zuki is one of the first moves karateka learn. The front fist is pulled back to generate power as the other fist thrusts forward with a straight arm. At the same time, the attacking karateka steps forward into the move.

3 Yoko Geri (Side Kick)

It takes excellent balance and quick, fluid movements to perform a good side kick, or *yoko geri*. The karateka brings her knee up high, twists sideways, and then thrusts her leg forward from the side. The striking area is the heel or the side of the foot.

MIND AND BODY

Karate is about improving the mind and body and getting them to work together.

Pause and Focus

Before beginning a karate class, students spend a few minutes calming and clearing their mind of thoughts other than karate. This is called meditating and is performed in a kneeling position, sometimes with the head lowered.

This karateka is in the kneeling position. He is wearing traditional karate robes from Japan.

The Three "Rs"

Respect for others and oneself is a vital part of the philosophy behind karate. There are two other important "R" words—routine and responsibility. Routine is something performed regularly. Karate practice and attitudes should become part of daily life.

Responsibility

Responsibility in karate means being in control of your words and actions in the *dojo* and elsewhere. Responsible karateka control their movements so they do not touch or strike a fellow student during training. They also do not use their karate skills outside the *dojo* to hurt or threaten.

Many karateka use kiai *to focus the power of the mind and improve the power of their body.*

"Karate may be referred to as the conflict within yourself, or a lifelong marathon that can be won only through self-discipline, hard training, and your own creative efforts."
Shoshin Nagamine (1907–97), legendary Okinawa karate instructor.

Power of Kiai

Skilled karateka can summon extra strength during training using a shout called *kiai. Kiai* is more than just a battle-cry, it is the release of focused energy from inside the body. Some karateka also use *kiai* to prepare themselves for difficult tasks.

TOP 10 KARATE MOVES 4 – 7

As karateka train hard in a *dojo*, they learn more complex moves. These require perfect concentration, form and timing.

4 **Gyaku-Zuki (Reverse Punch)**
Starting in the lunge punch position, the karateka punches with the left arm as she steps forward with the right leg (or the other way round). Performed with a thrust forward of both hips, *gyaku-zuki* is a fast, strong move.

5 **Knife-Hand Block**
Blocking moves (*uke*) are the main form of defense in karate. For a knife-hand block, the karateka uses a cutting action with a flat hand to deflect an attack, such as a straight punch to the head or body.

6 Jodan Uke

The *jodan uke* is a high block that uses a raised forearm, rising from the chest to above the head. It is designed to block an attack to the head or upper body.

7 Mawashi Geri

Mawashi geri is a powerful roundhouse kick. It starts with the karateka bringing his knee up to his hip with his lower leg folded in. Turning on his supporting foot, he snaps his kicking leg forward at the target. This can often deliver a winning blow in competitions.

KUMITE

Kumite or "partner work" are forms of sparring training or contests. Some kumite in a dojo involve two karateka making a series of agreed moves as training. Other forms of kumite are more competitive.

Competition Kumite

World Karate Federation (WKF) bouts last for three minutes for men and two minutes for women and juniors. Competitions take place on a 26 x 26ft (8 x 8m) mat. The action is incredibly intense as both karateka try to score points. Different moves score either one (ippon), two (nihan), or three (sanbon) points.

THE SEVEN SCORING AREAS

Areas that can be kicked or punched:
* Head
* Face
* Neck
* Abdomen
* Chest
* Back
* Side

Two competitors fight it out in a junior International Karate Friendship contest in Chiba, Japan.

Free Sparring

Free sparring (*jiyu-kumite*) in competition or the *dojo* sets opponents against each other to test their basic skills and to help teach them awareness, observation, and reactions. For juniors and all except the most experienced karateka, padded safety helmets, footwear, and gloves are compulsory.

Winning

Officials judge whether a move scores based on many factors, including timing. The karateka with the most points at the end of the bout wins. A bout can be stopped early if a competitor gets eight points ahead—he or she is declared the winner.

The referee awards the win to Ameen Tebib (Tunisia) in his kumite match against Tamer Abdel Raouf (Egypt) at the 2007 Asian Games.

IN COMPETITION

Karate may not yet be an Olympic sport, but karate competitions are held all over the world. Here are some of the most important events:

European Championships
Held every year since 1966, the Karate European Championships now has 17 different events. The 2009 tournament was held in Zagreb, in Croatia.

Asian Games
Karate has been a popular part of the Asian Games since 1994. There are team and individual events, and six weight divisions for men's *kumite* and four for women's.

The Asian Games are held every four years; the next games will be in 2010 in the Chinese city of Guangzhou.

Japan's Tetsuya Furukawa took gold in the individual kata at the 2006 Asian Games.

World Championships

The World Championships is the ultimate karate competition. It is organized by the World Karate Federation (WKF) and is held every two years. The 2008 WKF World Championships was held in Tokyo, in Japan.

THE FIRST WORLD CHAMPIONS

The first World Championships in Tokyo, Japan, in 1970 contained just two events—an individual competition and a team competition, both for men only. Japan scooped all three team medals, although their "E" team won gold and their "A" team finished with no medals!

TOP 10 KARATE MOVES 8—10

Surprise is a vital weapon in karate and the back kick and palm heel strike can be unexpected. Sometimes, a combination of moves can also surprise an opponent.

8 Shotei Uchi (Palm Heel Strike)

Palm heel strikes can be used to attack the stomach or head. With a firm wrist, the arm is thrust toward the target, snapping in then out like the strike of a snake. The padded bottom part of the palm, known as the heel, is the impact area with the fingers and thumb pulled back.

9 Ushiro Geri (Back Kick)

Ushiro geri was designed as a self-defense move when attacked from behind. The karateka turns his back to the direction of the kick, looks over his shoulder, and thrusts his kicking foot back with the heel leading.

10 Block and Backfist

In sparring competitions, karateka try to make their moves in combinations. Some involve a block to stop an opponent's attack, followed immediately by a strike. One such combination is to block an opponent's punch and then attack with a backfist. The fist is snapped out in a straight line so that the back of the hand connects.

FAMOUS KARATEKA

To be a great karateka takes dedication, skill, spirit, and great ability. Here are three famous karateka from around the world.

The One and Only

A 10th-dan black belt is the highest rank possible in karate. Hirokazu Kanazawa (born 1931) from Japan is the only living person in the world to be one! He started with judo but took up karate as a teenager.

Hirokazu Kanazawa studied under Gichin Funakoshi (page 6).

"The most important points of my teaching are breathing, movement, and timing." *Hirokazu Kanazawa*

Hawaii's History Maker

In 2002, Hawaii's Elisa Au became the first American woman to win a World Championship title. She repeated the feat in 2004 in the *kumite* sparring, over 130 pounds (60 kg) division, and came second at the 2005 World Games—all by the age of 24!

Elisa Au (right) faces up to Yadira Lira of Mexico during the Titan Games held in California.

Kata Champion

Italy's Luca Valdesi is the undisputed world number one at *kata*. Famous for his fast yet precise movements, he has won a staggering eight European Championships in a row (2000–07), two World Championships, and won the gold medal in the 2009 Italian Open. He has notched up a total of 87 gold medals!

"Every time that I train, I always attempt to give the maximum...It's my idea of karate." *Luca Valdesi*

Luca Valdesi performs a move from a kata at the Italian Open Championships in 2006.

GLOSSARY

blocks
Moves used to stop an opponent's punch or kick from striking their intended target area.

bout
A karate contest, usually a *kumite* sparring contest, between two people.

compulsory
Something that you must do.

dachi
Stances.

dan
The rank or level of a person practicing karate.

dojo
A training hall for karate and other martial arts.

geri
The Japanese word for kicking in karate.

gi
A special outfit worn when performing karate.

kata
A series of movements.

kiai
The shout you make as you perform a move or strike an opponent.

kumite
Sparring when two people perform.

ju-jitsu
A Japanese martial art.

martial arts
Different fighting sports.

meditating
Relaxing and clearing thoughts from your mind so you can concentrate.

occupied
An area of one country where another country has taken control.

philosophy
A set of beliefs or aims about life, and ways of thinking and acting.

sensei
A karate teacher or instructor.

stances
How you stand, position your feet, and balance your weight.

zuki
The Japanese word for punching in karate.

FURTHER INFORMATION

BOOKS

There are lots of instruction books available on karate. Check out your local library for books that suit you. The only way to really learn, though, is by joining a karate school.

Learn Karate
J. Allen Queen (Sterling Publishing, 2000)
A really good guide for beginners to the basic techniques involved in karate, with step-by-step series of images.

Karate
Sanette Smit (New Holland, 2001)
A colorful photographic guide to karate techniques and philosophy with dozens of color photographs.

Karate-Do: My Way of Life
Gichin Funakoshi (1997)
A short but amazing book about the life of the founder of Shokotan Karate, it's packed with little nuggets of wisdom and sayings.

DVDs AND MOVIES

Some of these movies are not suitable for all ages:

Simply Karate (Mark Richardson, Hinkler Books / Penton Overseas Inc, 2004)
This package contains a 64-page book and a DVD of basic karate moves, tips, and techniques. Just perfect to get your mind ready for a trip to a karate club.

The Karate Kid (John G. Avildsen, 1984)
Sure, it's old and a bit corny, but any kid into karate has to see *The Karate Kid*, even just once. Look out for the sequels, *KK II* and *III* and the 1994 movie, *The Next Karate Kid*, which starred Hilary Swank as a young karateka.

Shotokan Karate–A Beginner's Guide (Hosted by *Sensei* Jonathan Bolt, 2007)
Features moves performed in slow-motion to help beginners–and even comes with traditional Japanese background music!

WEB SITES

http://www.wkf.net/
Homepage of the World Karate Federation, this site has karate news, a calendar of events, championship results, and videos and picture galleries all to do with karate.

http://www.theshotokanway.com
This excellent web site is absolutely packed with articles, interviews, and features, including a large beginners section and a calendar of events. Set aside plenty of hours to surf these web pages.

http://www.karateworld.org
This is the web site for the World Karate Federation, the biggest organization involved in karate.

http://www.akakarate.com
The American Karate Association is to be one of the largest martial arts associations in the U.S.A., with members in almost every state. The site tells you about everything from tournament information to training aides.

Every effort has been made by the Publisher to ensure that these web sites contain no inappropriate or offensive material. However, because of the nature of the Internet, it is impossible to guarantee that the contents of these sites will not be altered. We strongly advise that Internet access is supervised by a responsible adult.

INDEX